AFTER ALL TOMORROWS' AFTER PARTIES

BY

MICHAEL WILSON

for William Campbell

THE KNIVES FORKS AND SPOONS PRESS
NEWTON-LE-WILLOWS

Published in the United Kingdom in 2010
by The Knives Forks And Spoons Press,
10 Avocet Close,
Newton-le-Willows,
Merseyside,
WA12 9RE.

ISBN 978-1-907812-16-3

Acknowledgements: 'The ECT Poem', 'Lucia Joyce', and 'Lot 48' previously appeared in *Poetry S Z*, '1968' was published by *Mental Virus*, and *Pipeline* were kind enough to include 'Untitled' in their organ. Many thanks to the editors involved.

Michael Wilson would like to give particular thanks to the Islington Mill Art Academy, who supported him during the writing process of this book.

CONTENTS

Introduction

These poems are full of the kind of inner fire that burns without causing scars. They take off from ordinary life into a galaxy of thought and experience that connects with the world at an oblique angle. There is an energy to these poems that is always on the verge of stumbling over itself and falling on its face; but it never does.

Michael Wilson has survived. He has, to quote DH Lawrence, come through. He has been through the experience of mental illness, through ECT and recovery, and he has lived to be become a poet. Like Ginsberg, he now channels his deep thoughts into lines and sentences, verses and whole poems. He tries to walk in the franked world with a naked mind, and to live as honestly as possible in a dishonest world.

There is a kind of poetry that is very polite, that sits down and drinks cups of tea in a kind of grey misery; but Michael Wilson does not do polite. Neither, however, does he do the kind of show-business 'outrage' of the professional ranter. These poems have been thought through and felt; they are political in that they proclaim a spiritual freedom for the soul of the underclass. They are also deeply personal, but not 'confession.' They are street poems for those who are looking from the gutter to the stars.

His precursors are Blakean, Wildean poets, like Lawrence and Ginsberg, like Hart Crane and Neruda. They are not perfect little boxes to put on a shelf with the other ornaments. They deserve to be read aloud, loudly.

Steven Waling

The ECT Poem

Ward Round Monday 10.30am
A ladder to somewhere else drawn on my arm
The days give each thought a bitter aftertaste
The terrible spun gold in my veins has finally been bled away
As you were my boy
But the dark always looks stranger with a keener sight
Surrounded by gluey eyes that try to scratch any meaning
From words and words, written over and over
On the same scrap of paper till the ink sweats from the page
The Doctor speaks from behind a shuffle of notes
"you see, we can't get there from here but I think it's time to see what we can call upon"
Something speaks for me
And he tells me the treatment will begin very soon
Once he regained his sense and the shape of his tongue
Tim tells us all a ghost story
How if you change your thinking, if you try and get off the gurney
They strap you down so they can safely feed icy water into your veins
To freeze the life inside you
He tells me what the letters mean
"you were tricked, my friend,
"but don't worry, it's just like sleeping, except you wake so much more tired

The days stalk the walls like shadows
My time is spent in circles
Orbiting the thought
On an ever shortening leash
The centre of all this is a dark hearted sun
I sweat out my dreams
And spend the daylight hours shitting out my fears
Until they tell me it's time to go
Hold your head, you're the lucky one

On the gurney, the ceiling glides over my eyes
The nurse looks down, affection and distance etch–a–sketched across his expression
Ward, corridor, lift, corridor, prep room

Until they inject the coldness into my hand
And I count back through every mistake I've ever made
They drop the curtain so I never see
The metal hands that pushed sparks into my mind

And I come back in the middle of his sentence
The world in front of me the size of a postage stamp
He plonks breakfast on a table in front of me
And my mind struggles into the clothing of thought
Come on, he says, back to the halfway house
Only five more treatments to go

"Each time I see you, you seem more... alive"
Became familiar words from visitors
carrying goodwill in brightly coloured bundles
Visits are no longer conducted through cottonmouth sentences
And layers of blankets that muffled down everything to a murmur
They told me at the last Ward Round
I'd get out of intensive care soon
The marvel of a Monday morning
I traded my memory for this place to turn its back on me
A life to come as full as a harvest moon
And eyes that have seen the things we hide from ourselves
Only to know the reason why
Shocked back into life and slotted back into the world
Complete

1968

The sun never really sets on television
Watching their flames
Flicker grey figurines across the walls
As their torn fingers rip up the cobblestones
To find the forgotten beach beneath
And across the copper green teeth houses
The ceilings are filled with the light of sulphured words
Until their hallowed, hollowed shapes
Can't be pulled from their place on the ancient walls of our cities
Built only years ago
But I can only know of our time
Through the eyes of our enemies
Who say our cloth cheeked message
Spoken through an acid tongue
Is the simple binary mind
The single tracked play of the young
While we choked down the glib one liners
Of Marx, Lennon, and Jagger
These newly franked thoughts
Broken across the back of It's tongue
To take down the dreamless spires and darkened towers
Dusky corridors and strangled wires
Of this careless world we never knew
And as the TV set shields me from the sun that sets outside
I wonder if there's a single thread of myself
Found in the folds and bright hues
Of the glimmering figurines
Whose polythene colours
Play through the screen
In their drab, dank black and white
Minds lost between the sheets
Of their bright shinning books
And clenched teeth of their sex
To line the university halls
With a history only old as

The soft skin of their hands will allow
With shoulders as slight as a chance that what plays from those shallow hips
Could ever be enough
To mean more than the weightless sedation
Of a simple pastime
And the way we judge the cold metallic touch
Of a world we try and burn to white
A world we never knew
Will blacken the sands beneath our feet
With something much darker
Than even the desperate voices
That share our most blistered paper dreams.

For all the songs that pull you through

The dawn chorus never speaks beyond the steps of Heaven
But we are all pieced together from the same scraps of a night sky
That backlights that same song that keeps playing in your ears
Whether the world makes a sound or not

In your hometown
There's nowhere else to run
Memory echoes every footstep
You walk past everyone you've ever been

Still with half a breath like someone else
And one eye trained on yourself
Waiting for the sky's next trick
And your next blind leap of logic

When the persistent little radio that's been tugging on your ears for attention
Suddenly comes good and recognition flicks on before its first bar falls fully formed
And feeling flows through your body and blood like the speeding weather high above
That looks calm and unaltered from a distance but hides an unbroken energy within

As you get older the songs that pull you through also come of age
Lift themselves from where they lay, sleeping in your head
And for a moment all the static ocean waves fall to a single line
All the white noise thoughts sharpen into a simple melody

And you realise you've walked these steps before
Between the beach floor and the attic streets
And this partly coloured world is not alone, so you surrender up your sense
And go by the solid grass brushed slope beneath your feet

So, you let your song's banner line colours catch an invisible eye
You let the sun above your head speak to you in word–like feelings you finally understand
You let the troubles that cling like damp clothing fall to pieces
And you find when the patterned chaos fades, your mind reclaims its central refrain

Pack up your footsteps in memory, one day you'll need to know where they led
Leave the songs that pull you through in a familiar place
Remember there is a song for every salvation, there is a place to receive every gentle breath
Follow yourself to the attic streets and walk home past everyone you've ever been

This Is It

Wandering In the steps of night
A bystander to the thoughts
I don't belong to
And I know the mirror clock
Will call time
And fall into that fattened hour
There's comfort in any comedown
It's just sometimes that's all I can see
When my mind slips from the tracks
And truckles into sometime less clunkysome
Each spackled thought brings a resolution
To a problem slaked of existence
By stumbletongue fingered revelations
A copy of a copy of its own copy
And fallen into an old way of thinking
But sometimes changed
And thoughts run faster
Than can be collected
My eyes spin under the weight of the street mop up all thought to hear the scene sickened words that fall like stars followed the needle streets through snatch throat sentences cut in two to mark gutters and stars a vagrant gesture starts slippery shocks of sentimentality and cars pass my sides breath on my skin on the street naked skin shivers between heaven and hell and this scratchy feeling in my soul deepens and widens and the whole world can hear me breathing and I want to throw up every word I've ever heard attic or basement and look for a language like mine pavements glisten cold this cold planet the sky stripped of finery carry the caring and the heartfully dead remember her words
Keep It Safe
Keep It Simple
Trying to cling to an epiphany I found some doublebacked hours ago that's been changing face every time it's words can be plucked from the sky and everything grinds to a hush somewhere in this city is a single open door and the crowds of angry teeth and sour tan breath crush onto the night and swallow up each nightlight thought inside my skin and between my eyes love and hate on different hands one foot curls in pleasure one in pain one look throw so lightly from a grazing eye litany of loss and but there is something dark and hardened in the shift of bodies from the hot breath clubs pour from inside groaning walls

carefully skitter through corners and take the city with them and I want to throw up every word I've ever heard but all I can do is spit a single ball of spit that hits the pavement and burrows deep deeper deeper

The room where Bowie wrote "Heroes"

I clambered down from the voice of resistance
Burning into spinning black vinyl like the needle sharp sun burns into your retina
But In this room its light is now strapped across my back
That showed me again
That the Berlin sun has a way of pushing back its own dark history
And its quiver light present
And in this room if evil knew itself
It would have found itself here
Now washed clean by music in the head, on the page, from the throat
A stolen kiss by a wall,
Berlin's greatest message is that you are only ever 24 hours or one truly great act
Away from total redemption
And to be a part itself of this choir of resistance
Singing from above the darkened shadows that danced on the ashes of their enemies
Real and imagined
The hastily gathered history that speaks to you through the patterned glass doors upstairs
Patched together from half finished conversations
Recorded within those walls and left to leak out slowly
To thicken and collect like time until each floor finally gave way
And now it fills out the corners of every room
Like sunlight
And so soon I'll clamber back upstairs
So in the womb like silence
When you can only hear your own voice
Coming back to you through a wire and a pair of headphones
You still find you're speaking to the entire world
And for once the song you hold in your throat comes out
Almost a carbon copy of the one in you once held in your head

Lucia Joyce (daughter of James Joyce)

the slumped book between the bed and the wall
between the bed and the wall the slumped book
it's cover shape it's dense material
typset it's cover shape
it's dense material typeset
is the focus of a sourceless mind when the mirror only bites
when the mirror only bites is the focus of a sourceless mind

my cottonmouth sentences
spoken in sleep
have a way of stumbling into this world

he carries his original sin
the way our land
was held in the silvery palm of the English

and the lamp light shine doesn't know
many of his words are
half closed doors
strange hand me downs
the thoughts that run from this room to his
but never return

and this night book
fallen between the bed and the wall
was a meandering risk he took
greater than my mind could ever close itself around

somewhere lost among these words
was a chance, fading yellowing and browned
any time it was shown the brightening daylight
to be something other than his fearsome muse
more than a broken lover for his grovelling soft headed subjects

but the real words
are the ones I don't know how to form
never mind let go
to spin strange patterns
across this arcing room

so soon I'll sleep for him
I'll dream for him
to wake with fistfuls of things for him
to fool them again into believing the trick of the strangeness of his lucidity

and the reason of our insanity
is the slumped space between me and him
instead of the shared resting place
of the tender footprints of our most beautiful boundless self

All these things that I have seen

city road turn their backs into rivers
the flesh falls from her face
bodies assemble in the night
the scars that cut into this town
become woodland desirelines
the cage of the mind
is beautiful
and when it opens a crack
all heaven breaks loose
and songs sound like flags
colours you've never seen
but as natural as the shift
in the light when night rises into morning
everthing you have seen is precious
and you can find out
there's a man who filled in
a planning permission application
for a castle in the sky
but you can't believe a thing
until the dozers roll right in
and all your visions
are safe for now
in the killing room
all your yesterdays
are safely held
in your mother's womb
memory bothers
trying to remember why
are pieces of people you used to know
whispering in your ear
'cause they know the thoughts
that creep beneath the door with the morning light
the only reason they don't know
they belong to you
is cause they share them too

and in the blind of morning
you watch the clock count
through all your mistakes
every zero is only the start of something new
until it winds up chasing its own tail
and you find yourself back at the begin
only to begin again with nothing to show for itself
except for the clink of loose change in your head
that's never quite enough
to get exactly what you want
but just enough to make you think about it instead
all these things i've seen
serve some kind of purpose
i just don't know what it is yet
like dreams part remembered in the blinking sunlight
once looked at
they simply bleed away
and maybe all we will ever see, will ever hear
like life
is the space between the dying of one lullaby
and the start of another

An ode to Autumn

Deep down in yourself
Deep down in your coat
The autumn falls before your eyes
Smoke perspires from car exhausts
And the street sounds silent in your head
Watching the traffic find its way,
from safe inside the hem of a hood
The unlit cigarette burns a hole in your hand
As you take the world in,
A stage set street at a time

Your thoughts are wrapped up in pretty paper
Round numbers and letters and how they fit their clothing
In the wooliness of your mind
You had to train yourself to doublethink
A single line when added to
Creates a picture you can just make out
In the dark horse sky
A sky that maps this world
All true intention pushed underfoot
The leaves
And all the deadness of past summer
Crushed underfoot

You hear a beating memory in your head
That from your past, autumn never means you harm
The curled blur of street lights
Match the fuzziness in your logic
Walks with you
An elegant procession of thoughts that play to beat the band
A foresight that this winter won't bite too hard
Cause it knows its own mortality
A backlit sight that summer leaves a mark or two on your skin,
but won't do what it's told, it won't change your life,
this time around.

You walk
Back to your home the rest of the world in front
The street smells of everything and nothing at once
While the moon makes it's once sightly appearance
A smile like benevolent stupidity
A smile like a patriarch not a sister
A father for you to figure out your thoughts
And for this moment your happiness won't get away
The day comes back to you
In the soft grip of night
That Autumn holds its lover lightly
As it lets the summer leave you
Feeds you and clothes you in your own colours
The halfway secret shine of Autumn is held in the single change of a skin

Lot 48

Just now I saw a woman's back as she fed an empty Shredded Wheat packet
Into a red post box on Oxford Road
Near the Lidl and the Superdrug
In a bulged carrier bag strapped to her wrist
Were egg cartons and such like

Her clothes didn't look strange but her hair gave away her age
I didn't stop to watch
But instead fell into an empty pub
To write these words, which seems so much worse
Asked the barman to carry the tea to my table
Cause even after all these years my hands still shake

I wondered about her serenity
Maybe between the knotted ends of furious thoughts
But there was something in her calm determination
That said to me that for her, for one moment at least, all was well in the world
But less so the 2nd, 3rd, 4th deposit she made
I even thought she might be a vandal
About to throw in a lighted match
But there's enough tinder in there already
I wondered about the clichéd reasons
TV presenter voices, radios clicked off and eyes of strangers, got angry with myself
Then thought of the cliché that these things are usually true

I had wondered for a fleeting shameful thought
About taking her hand and leading her to the bright lights and green metal chairs of the nearby A+E
As stupid an idea as those who kneel beery breathed by the homeless in the cold and give them a list of things to save themselves

I'd probably just distress her, a simple mantra to repeat until such dumb heroic thoughts faded away
And soon the mundane thoughts of how to fill an evening begin to play out instead

So soon it'll bleed white from memory
Until I see another member of her not so exclusive club
And there she'll be, a figure to cut out and keep
To speak of in pubs and living rooms
When relevance comes along

So her fate it seems in all is whether we believe in good strong voiced endings
Or long tattered beginnings
The only real connection here isn't with me and her
Not right now anyway
But whether any or even every other person that's seen her before
Leaves the road and follows the same dead end path as mine

Who Ended the Troubles?

It was us, the chemical generation
That saw an end to the Troubles
Fresh eyed from the revelation
There was another world
On which to raise their future children
Away from the machine gun rattle of flags
And all those semtex words
A flame without a fuse
Art and voice put to better use
So the bombmaker and the quartermaster
The fodder and the spies
Realised it was much easier
To smuggle pills than bullets
So they sold the chemical generation their freedom back to them
At a vastly inflated price
But it was never about them
It was only ever about us
All that cloth minded symbolism
Closer in thought, word, and deed
To each other
Than to anyone who claim to lead them
There isn't a family that hasn't had it's victim
There isn't a family that hasn't been touched
And yet we hope to struggle on
Despite books of history
Housed in walls of gravestones
Beacuse the Northern Irish, each and everyone
Knows the strength they fed on
When it was all peace lines and punishment beatings
Protection rackets, snipers, and executions
Would be the same inner strength
On which to build that other world.

Life in a mortal universe

Wake from your sleep while I scrabble the foothills have I noticed the words yet the internal dialogue that runs beneath the sheets it creates words faster than I can make them doublestitched from scraps of the day sky clouded conversations that the rest of the room clusters in attendance keeps me from sleep the clutter of the day the knife and fork conversations that clatter from concave tongues shine with a kind of dull dishwater mind refracts the colour and pallor of thoughts that creep between the cracks between the minutes of the infant hours and the drumbeat of my heart begins to spread the vibrations and the sound of the ocean that roars in my head keep me further from sleep and no matter how I shift my soul I can't get the sound to cease oh well counting the time until I can quit the bed and the last three hours and change and smoke a shivering cigarette in the gloom of my mood that rises from my body and fills the room like darkness and then crawl back in hoping that the bed doesn't recognise me this time and the thoughts will let me be until then the cars scrape by their owners a world away all the billion and one miracle of a moment I want nothing to do with the heroes and the villains of the past few presents enter the room all the fuck ups all the stupid things all the cursed opportunities all the things said and done to death play on scratchy acetate a never ending run out groove the insomnia is on a roll back the hours and I realise I can trace my thoughts back like a beam and fight the urge to check the clock cause it never ends well that one and the realisation that there are countless people stretched across this city who find themselves the same but it makes me feel no different as I shift into my 75th position and fast slow thoughts are keeping me from changing from lying a quarter of an inch above the bed and earlier the road seemed so lifeless on the long thread home and the houses looked like monopoly pieces and for a moment the whole world seemed made up not imaginary but created not just the streets and the board game pieces but all the people inside and something scrapes away at me through a duvet that gets itchier by the thought and I think about getting out of bed and fixing a joint but the cold keeps me chained to the hope that sleep might drip in soon and the next day would be like another life

Wake Up

and all the broken heart liquor
didn't save you from the morning
instead it dropped you right in it
from a great height
and left you there
to fend for yourself

and another day weighed down across your shoulders
one of those where the sun can barely lift its head to shine
finding new avenues for her old words to travel
leaving and returning to the same thought like the tide
that once you'd reached the bottom
there's nowhere else to go

and you put her words up to the lamplight shine
you see through them
to what she really said
and when you turned it off and fell into bed
those words glow in the corner of the room while you sleep
and waited for you to wake again

and the early summer sun can make you feel
like you're someone different
but we know better than the fuck around
don't we?
a life so lonely
that it's company that's the pain

in the corner of a thought
in a room by the edge of her voice
in a space beneath her breath
in a small black medicine box
lost from your eye in shadow
was a word dropped softly into your dreaming ear

and in the sprawl of the afternoon
you find your thoughts follow the slow sweep
of the clock hand until they find their way back again
but today they seem to breathe slow and easy
they say pain finds its own level
if that's true, then so must joy

and your word stained lips fall into a smile
that every new minute, marked into the ground by all our hands
opens up the sky above your head by another inch
and all the broken heart liquor can fend for itself
cause this time, you can let yourself hear her final words slip away at last
before you allow yourself to sleep it off

Antrim Hollywell Psychiatric Hospital Intensive Care Acute Ward 10

the windows are obscured by outside
the grey sticklesick carpet sucks at my shoes
at the far end of the killing room
has changed shape and stayed there
but the tortured cigarette burns along its floor
have left a pattern on the backs of my eyelids
at night i sometimes wake to find
the bloodening flood of torch light
on my sweat covered bed
the very voice of plod
hisses "sleep"
and the little world clicks off

everything here is nailed in
in the pan headed canteen
knives are the last to be laid
all conversation, like clothing, like thought, like action, like reason
is static grey
except for during the red shift
when pain creeps under fingernails
and everything turns outside in
then words crawl the walls
or a scream rises and falls like a resting breath
here
the walls are bugged
and the water's drugged
and the captors' eyes hypnotise

at first i'd spend days within the starch sheets
closed eyes can keep you safe it seems
wrapped in itchy cotton wool
waiting for the sinking sound of footsteps
and at night here the others clutch a playing card to their chests
dreams of sainthood and fire escapes
in the darkness the sometime sound of a tin box opening from another bed

makes me throw up
as time falls on i begin to start conversations i can't keep
every walk on part visitor to the tv room shifts very walls around inside
sense explains itself in 3 second broadcasts from the world outside
then folds back like silence, like space, like inaction, like reason
into static grey

they have to flush out the sweetness they gave me
cause it makes me sick
living through the chill
with nothing in my veins
but weak water valium and headache pills
living for visits
and the first joke i crack open
just to see what happens next
yesterday they asked me if i'd let them try their last trick
here in the dull of each dawn all it holds
is all it is
and all it is
all it was
is time until the blue shift
and the little world clicks on again
and leaves me with the greatest gift of all
to be able to fully realise
that life is beautiful

Untitled

Be careful with that cigarette in your hand
Watching the honeymooners play their limbs up to the night
I see others peel away the edges of their tin foil heart and devour all they find
The push and pull of human skin, the twist and turn of puckered bone
In it together and all that, the glint of teeth and smell of sweat
Light filters through fingers while the strange thoughts creep noiselessly through your head
Figures hunch in desperate drafts, and at your feet are all the misery of tomorrow
But for now there's still a few hours to spare
On the big screen staccato sharp images are punctuated by clunky soled adverts for this and that, but after a while it all crashes together so you pay no mind
All the colours pass your eyes, lost in themselves, striving to be a different shade
Magnetic tattoos and glowsticks, Vicks and the dense damp air of poppers, and you still get tracers from that cigarette in your hand, as the prophetic and dumb grind thoughts break in, enter your head and destroy all they come across. And you know there isn't long, you can hear it, feel it threaded in the thrusts of arms around you and the DJ plucks and plucks at the music until it peaks and drops everyone into tomorrow.
You push away from the press of heat of the tent and the sky outside quivers between night and day. All around you are Lowry's matchstick men, shambling past each other, trying to piece together their own concentration and sense of purpose, kicking through masses of rubbish and at your feet are dead plastic fires, flat plastic cups, empty plastic bottles and plastic bank bags, they stretch away from you over acres and acres. And you don't want to be here as all those litmus paper tongues an hour ago were so sugar sweet will be turning to acid and your mind's tired self slips into the murky cool of a comedown, and something you didn't want to think about tugs at a sleeve of thought.
When suddenly, the thin lying form of the horizon brightens and a dilated pupil of a sun breaks through the rubbish strewn ground.
And the sun brightens the corners of everyone's faces as your mind is jolted to the present for just one blessed moment, as you can feel the grind of the earth underneath your feet. But it's the speed you notice most but it seems at once longer and shorter than that. And the sky is a beautiful blue eyed boy and some part of it gets lodged in your throat and stays throughout the day, but for now it's time to go home.
After all, life is a wonderful waste of time.

ABOUT ISLINGTON MILL ART ACADEMY

Islington Mill Art Academy is a free self-organised art school based in Manchester, UK. It was set up in 2007 by a group of art foundation students, dissatisfied with the quality and standards in University fine art courses open to them at that time.

The Academy exists to experiment with what an education in art can be, where it can take place and how it can be paid for. It is open to anyone who would like to be an artist and who is interested in taking responsibility for, and direction of the way in which they intend to do this. The artists in the group take all of the decisions related to their personal learning process and put these decisions into practice themselves.

The group invites visiting artists to talk about their work and to give feedback on the work of artists from the Academy on a regular basis. Academy artists organise residencies and research trips to other parts of the UK and abroad for all members of the group. In 2008, we visited Glasgow, Bristol and Sheffield and held residencies in Berlin and the Lake District.

Islington Mill Art Academy
Studio 101
Islington Mill
James St.
Salford
Greater Manchester
M3 5HW

+44 (0) 7917714369

www.ingramcontent.com/pod-product-compliance
Ingram Content Group UK Ltd.
Pitfield, Milton Keynes, MK11 3LW, UK
UKHW012252290726
14090UKWH00016B/603

9 781907 812163